Business Employee Discipline

B. Vincent

Published by RWG Publishing, 2021.

BUSINESS EMPLOYEE DISCIPLINE

First edition. May 16, 2021.

Written by B. Vincent.

Also by B. Vincent

Affiliate Marketing
Affiliate Marketing
Affiliate Marketing

Standalone
Business Employee Discipline
Affiliate Recruiting
Business Layoffs & Firings
Business and Entrepreneur Guide
Business Remote Workforce
Career Transition
Project Management
Precision Targeting
Professional Development
Strategic Planning
Content Marketing
Imminent List Building
Getting Past GateKeepers
Banner Ads

Bookkeeping
Bridge Pages
Business Acquisition
Business Bogging
Marketing Automation
Better Meetings
Business Conflict Resolution
Conversion Optimization
Creative Solutions
Employee Recruitment
Startup Capital
Employee Mentoring
Followership
Servant Leadership
Human Resources
Team Building
Freelancing
Funnel Building
Geo Targeting
Goal Setting
Immanent List Building
Lead Generation
Leadership Course
Leadership Transition
LinkedIn Ads
LinkedIn Marketing
Messenger Marketing
New Management
Newsfeed Ads
Search Ads
Online Learning

Sales Webinars
Side Hustles
Split Testing
Twitter Timeline Advertising

Table of Contents

Business Employee Discipline

P aul Foster once said:

"Dealing with employee issues can be difficult, but not dealing with them can be worse".

And Steve Wynn warns us that:

"If you run a business, if you are responsible for a lot of people, you come to grips with the reality that you have to have discipline, you have to protect the enterprise."

And it's true!

Disciplining your employees is difficult to think about, but undeniably necessary.

If you want your workplace to remain a well-oiled machine, you'll need to correct problematic personnel from time to time but how can we be sure to handle this critical aspect of leadership and management the right way? What's the most effective way to correct reprimand, and even terminate an employee without negatively impacting workplace morale?

In this course, we're going to show you how to do exactly that.

A survey said that, '71% of workplaces reported disputes or conflicts in one year'.

Connecting to this, another survey said that:

"ABOUT 52% OF EMPLOYEES said that, 'They had witnessed one kind of misconduct in the workplace in a given year', and 36% of them said that, 'they witnessed two or even more kinds.'"

It goes without saying that conflict requires mediation, and often those end and punishments for 1 or 2 parties.

However, 58.3% of respondents in a given study disagreed with utilizing punishments to correct behavior.

These statistics show that mentoring is an increasingly important area that businesses should focus on.

Our course is going to consist of a series of critical discussion points. These are designed to cover this broad topic as thoroughly as possible to encourage growth in these vital areas and to facilitate a real and fruitful discussion within your organization about how you can each improve on this essential characteristic, both at work, and in your personal lives in general.

Some of these will be pretty lengthy, and some will be relatively straightforward and brief. At the very end of this roadmap comes the most important final step.

Do not skip this. This is the most important part of this training.

Discussion time!

When you finish this course, you need to spend at least an hour or so going over the questions we supply at the end as a group. Whoever's the head honcho in the group should designate a facilitator whose responsibility it is that each question is covered and then everyone time permitting, is able to have their say.... Make sure all contributions are valued, all suggestions considered, and all opinions respected.

So let's move into the first discussion point.

Disciplining Employees

This may not be readily apparent, but disciplining employees isn't exactly your supervisors' favorite pastime. Disciplining your employees isn't about being the top dog and letting everyone know it. Disciplining is done for the good of the employees and the work environment. Employee discipline sets an example and protects the business. Therefore, it's in the organization's best interest to create a communication channel which is consistent and clear regarding disciplining employees. It will be instrumental in avoiding lawsuits, especially for wrongful terminations.

Why do we need to discipline people anyway?

When employee behavior doesn't measure up to company standards, profits suffer, so does productivity and the work environment.

Discipline involves informing the employee about the issue or issues post haste and they should be given the chance to remedy it. Once you've gotten that squared away, follow the disciplinary process as prescribed by your organization's rules and regulations.

Most of the time, you'll find that instruction and correction is the case when it comes to disciplining employees.

As a supervisor, it's your duty to explain to the offending employee what areas or aspects they must improve on and propose solutions. You're also supposed to give them a reasonable period of time to implement the solutions. Only when serious misbehavior, such as physical assault or theft occurs, should you escalate to equally serious actions, such as immediate termination. If you're faced with such a case, you've got to go to the proper authorities and or associations.

Progressive Discipline

Disciplining employees is a difficult part of a leaders' job. Not many leaders enjoy doing so... but it is a necessary evil. When disciplining it's best to take the progressive approach. Most times when issues regarding employees crop up, the company usually goes through a process called **Progressive Discipline**. **Progressive Discipline** may be legally defensible, but having to go through the entire process may cost the company much in terms of productivity, time and profits.

One may have to weigh the resources being spent on the offending employee against hiring and training an entirely new employee.

Here's how it goes in order before that award of warning, the process may not be as straightforward as described here in.

The number of exchanges and time spent on each step may differ greatly depending on who you're disciplining:

1. Verbal warning or counseling.

1. Written warning,

1. Suspension.

1. Termination.

Stage One of Progressive Discipline:
Verbal warning:

As soon as a problem crops up, talk to the employee involved in the issue. Make sure to specifically state the issues you want to improve on and what solutions can be done in order to fix them. Do this tactfully and constructively. It would be ideal if you had a script for this stage. This step can also harbor a less formal disciplinary process.

For example: If an incident is small enough, you may do some quick course correcting.

If there's a need to meet multiple times in order to facilitate the disciplinary process, do so you must advise your employee is necessary. At this stage, you already need to start keeping track of what you discuss with your employees and ensure it's written down somewhere like a Word file to document the disciplinary process.

Stage two of Progressive Discipline:
Written Warning:

If the employee persists with their bad behavior, or less than optimal performance, or even if they take umbrage at being reprimanded in step one, give them a written warning. This warning must be detailed. It can be in digital or print form or perhaps even both. Write a formal letter or email explaining why you're dissatisfied with how the employee is conducting themselves. Best to cite particular things you'd previously discussed with the employee. As you've already noted in stage one, you may have to mention that they will be suspended or even terminated if they still haven't improved themselves after a given period of time.

Once this is done, send a signed copy of the written warning signed by yourself.... The person who's mediating the conflict of course, the neutral witness and the offending employee. In case the employee is confused about your guidance, you may give them a written copy of the documentation pertaining to the advice you'd given them.

Mid stage of Progressive Discipline

Final documentation:

Your offending employees still persisting. Use your documentation of the disciplinary process so far. Basically, you'll have to read a comprehensive list of the employee shortcomings, how they failed to achieve the benchmark and reprimands from the supervisor and what they were advised to do from the time the problem first came up. This isn't the end of the line for them though. The employees still got the rest of the process to make things right.

When documenting for the disciplinary process the necessary information required is as follows:

- The issues which need attention.

- The goals for improvement.

- Checkpoints for particular short term goals.

- And deadlines.

These are 4 bigger goals as well as a final or important goal.

1. Ensure that you organize all pertinent information.

1. Also ensure that in a separate file you have the information discussed in the disciplinary meeting,

1. Information and discussions with eyewitnesses or complainants.

1. And the offending employee.

All written statements exchanged, especially between the mediating manager and the offending employee. All documents relating to the complaint or issue, the supervisors report pertaining to their investigation on the problem and all records of any solutions proposed and or taken.

Step Three of Progressive Discipline

Suspension or Probation:

If the issue still persists to this point, it's time for a suspension without pay.

When you send a letter or an email of suspension, you must state in no uncertain terms that the employee will be at risk of further suspensions or terminations. If they don't improve themselves. Before you do the suspending best to talk it over with some HR professionals. A number of additional penalties alongside the suspension may be imposed as the management sees fit.

Examples of these are: Docking ones pay, continuous supervision by a manager or retraining the employee.

Stage Four of Progressive Discipline

Termination:

If you haven't achieved the desired results at this stage, and even with so many measures in place, termination may be an order. The termination meeting must be done in person. Not only this, but you need to have disciplinary processes documentation in order to outline everything relating to the process. The issues, the solutions from both the manager and the employee, and so forth.

Schedule the employee for a pre termination conference.

Outline the reasons for termination and a letter that serves as a call to the conference.

Once you've begun the conference, the employee must respond to the reasons for termination. Listen to them well and after you've got to deliberate on whether or not you'll carry out the termination, or simply give a penalty.

Quick pointers before you get started on the progressive discipline process. Now that you've got the basics of progressive discipline down, you need to make sure you're prepared to begin the process.

Here are some tips that will really smooth it over:

Get familiar with the law. management staff basically have free rein on how to deal with internal issues or conflicts but they've all got to be aware of the law. It broadly covers issues regarding workplace discipline.

Employers are advised to be cautious and thorough. So you may have a lawyer go over things with you to ensure that you don't miss anything.

Have everyone sign off on the company rulebook. Make sure that the rules of the company are clearly outlined in writing. Cover every detail you possibly can so your staff can act in the way you intend for them to. You may also read the rules out loud.

Get your managers on the same page when it comes to discipline. You've got to ensure that your managers are fully aware of company rules and regulations and how the law impacts them. This is to avoid legal trouble. managers have different leading styles. So what follows that they'll have different disciplining styles. managers should be consistent in handling transgressions.

Figure out how you'll dish out discipline. There are many approaches to disciplining your staff. So figure out if a punitive or a corrective approach is what you need for a given situation or impromptu course correction. Use the approach that you believe works best for your business, your personal comfort level, as well as the particular employee you have to convene with while speaking to the offending employee.

When disciplining be cautious because your employee can end up taking legal action against you. Employers aren't worried about discipline just because they hate confrontation. So keep these tips in mind.

Be clear, be very clear, be very clear and concise in your wording. You must reference the gravity of the issue, clearly define the problem in an understandable way when you speak to the employee, you've got to talk about the undesirable behavior and its impact on the organization.

Explain clearly and concisely to them why the behavior is an issue and why you want to do address it, and the employee will want to fix the issue of their own free will.

This is also an effort in using objective language.

Structuring your disciplinary speech in this manner will help the employee understand and it allows them the chance to take responsibility for themselves.

Avoid bringing your personal opinions into it, and you'll avoid sounding like you're attacking your employee. You may also provide physical evidence in case your employee tries to deny or refute your case.

Write it all down.

Right, every everything down.... Everything. Take note of everything you and the employee discuss when you have your private sit down. Make sure you have the details of aberrations in the employees' usual outputs or patterns. This can be correlated into a document which will be proof when asked why you believe there's an issue with the employee.

After sorting it out, send this summary document to the offending employee, and ask them if they've got any qualms with it. Having you be aware of company guidelines, take note that a manager should review your documentation work, especially before you terminate someone.

However, termination isn't your only option. You may have the employee resign, transfer or be demoted. You'll want to have the proper documentation supporting you in case drastic measures are required.

Get your facts straight. Know the details of the situation and base your methods on that. So if you've got a simple performance issue, you can manage it with some coaching. If you're dealing with an employee who's willfully doing malicious actions, chances are you'll need to be much harder on them. You need to have all the information surrounding the issue in one file.

So before you end the meeting, or even during it, check if you overlooked anything. You have to understand the situation in its entirety or you may make bad calls that result in best in the employee opposing you for your poor decision or at worst, a lawsuit.

Check if the employees' behavior was goaded by some sort of outside factor.

Ask them if there were any outside factors or problems giving them difficulty. Or if there are any people inciting the undesirable behavior.

Your rulebook is your shield. Make sure everyone knows the drill. The company rulebook will greatly help with this. Ensure that the policies contained therein cover an abundance of situations. Use the rulebook to guide how you'll deal with disciplining an employee. The usual policy organizations follow is progressive discipline. It doesn't have to use a particular schedule. So the amount of time you pour into each stage depends on the nature of the issue. Your rulebook is made of paper.

So bend the rules. Follow the company's rules and regulations but do so within reason. There should be allowances for the unexpected. Discipline your staff fairly in accordance with the rules but don't be overly strict. Your company mostly has free rein when it comes to disciplining your employees. So bend the rules as you see fit.

Make sure to consistently apply the rules while being fair and impartial with your judgments. Also, discuss with the offending employee about the issue in private.

Speak from the heart. Say it like you mean it.

Focus on positive growth and not threats.

Correction helps in the long term while threats will alienate the employee from you because you're inspiring fear. You must provide clear steps towards a longer term solution and you should also write this down in documentation. People will consciously or subconsciously want to improve themselves and become a better person, and by extension, a better person in your organization. Help your employee through their journey of self-correction. You and the employee should understand everything thoroughly. There shouldn't be any room for confusion or misunderstandings. If the employee isn't clear on something, make it clear for them.

Do this and the employee can realize how the behavior or action got to this point, and perhaps even help them find the root cause of the issue.

Start using positive discipline and compliments as soon as you can. Apply positive feedback as soon as possible. You can't just wait for a few days to praise your employee for their positive effort and good behavior. Let them know you're grateful to the employee for hearing you out the moment you finished a conversation with them. This will enhance the bond you have with that employee. The discipline you dealt won't feel so harsh when you're so invested in helping the employee change for the better.

Some other things to avoid when disciplining employees. If you're a manager, there's no way to avoid having to discipline your employees sooner or later. If you dread doing it, don't worry so much. Many supervisors don't particularly enjoy having to confront their staff either, but it's still part of your job to deal with it.

When disciplining most of the time, it's to correct instead of punish, you don't have to immediately get the metaphorical paddle out the moment someone doesn't do their work the way you intend. People want to be good. People want to succeed, whether actively or subconsciously.

Here are some things to do to avoid escalating the situation when disciplining your employees. Don't check it out. Don't skirt around or disregard the issue. No matter how much you dislike confronting someone, you're the boss. To alleviate the intimidation factor, focus on helping your employee be the best version of themselves.

Speak to the offending employee as appear. Speak to the offending employee on equal terms. Treat them well. Even as you're talking about the action or behavior you find disagreeable. Once you've laid out the basic details, you'll need to actively involve the employee in problem solving. Ask them for ways to solve the issue instead of forcing the solution on them, they get to choose the solution for themselves.

Don't razz your employees. You can't discipline the employee in full view of every person in the company.

Not only is this grounds for a legal complaint, you risk embarrassing them. You must have private meetings when disciplining your employees. However, you may also have another manager in the room to serve as a witness. Stay calm, cool and collected. Take your emotions out of the conversation. Be logical and calm while you're disciplining your offender. If you do this, there's very little chance of you escalating the tension. If you start off the discussion in a composed manner, chances are the offending employee will follow your tune. You cannot conduct discipline when the person you're talking to is too inflamed to carry on an investigative discussion. an ounce of prevention and all that.

Have regular private meetings with your staff. One on one time will help you sniff out any issues before they grow into something particularly troublesome. This also strengthens your employees' relationship with you and your company as well and will motivate them to work harder.

Be the shining example. Do what your employees should be doing and this sets a precedent for them. Your actions will establish discipline without having to say much or anything at all.

Disciplining employees is good and all, but in order to lessen conflicts with problems within the company before they even arise.

Here are some tips:

Get active. Get everyone's blood pumping. If you add a physical fitness activity to the work day, people will become far more productive than if they hadn't started their day with some blind calisthenics.

Have employees show off what they're doing. The objective of this is to motivate your other employees, not to make them feel bad about how little or how slowly they're doing their jobs. do this right, and everyone will end up being more conscious about how they go about their day. If you show off their tasks, you can keep track of these tasks by using a whiteboard, or perhaps online tools.

Get an operation workflow going: The workflow needs to detail tasks and also the deadline of the task. Aside from this, you'll need to physically check in on your people regularly, as well as the tasks they're working on. This can be expedited with online tools or applications.

Engage everyone and discipline will follow. Establish a system of regular status reports of everyone's accomplishments. This forces each employee to hold themselves accountable for their work ethic.

Have weekly reports so it doesn't feel like too much of a hassle for your staff.

Give your employees a free lunch as a treat. Your employees won't need to go too far or take too long to get their midday meals, which takes out a potential source of stress and serves as an extra perk of working for your company.

Have a coaching or counseling memo ready-made and on hand. This will streamline everything and ensure the process isn't too cumbersome or too laborious.

You'll want all possible areas of concern laid out in the form. This will include:

1. Expectations.

1. And solutions.

Establish regular performance evaluations for your employees. That is, if you haven't already. Its goal is to guide the behavior of employees as well as become a bonding activity.

With regular evaluations, you will motivate your employees into working harder for the company.

And now it's discussion time. The most important part of this training whoever's the head honcho in the group should designate a facilitator whose responsibility it is, that each of the questions you see on your screen is covered and then everyone time permitting is able to have their say.

Make sure all contributions are valued. All suggestions considered and all opinions respected.

Don't miss out!

Visit the website below and you can sign up to receive emails whenever B. Vincent publishes a new book. There's no charge and no obligation.

https://books2read.com/r/B-A-QWUO-TVVOB

BOOKS 2 READ

Connecting independent readers to independent writers.

Also by B. Vincent

Affiliate Marketing
Affiliate Marketing
Affiliate Marketing

Standalone
Business Employee Discipline
Affiliate Recruiting
Business Layoffs & Firings
Business and Entrepreneur Guide
Business Remote Workforce
Career Transition
Project Management
Precision Targeting
Professional Development
Strategic Planning
Content Marketing
Imminent List Building
Getting Past GateKeepers
Banner Ads

Bookkeeping
Bridge Pages
Business Acquisition
Business Bogging
Marketing Automation
Better Meetings
Business Conflict Resolution
Conversion Optimization
Creative Solutions
Employee Recruitment
Startup Capital
Employee Mentoring
Followership
Servant Leadership
Human Resources
Team Building
Freelancing
Funnel Building
Geo Targeting
Goal Setting
Immanent List Building
Lead Generation
Leadership Course
Leadership Transition
LinkedIn Ads
LinkedIn Marketing
Messenger Marketing
New Management
Newsfeed Ads
Search Ads
Online Learning

Sales Webinars
Side Hustles
Split Testing
Twitter Timeline Advertising

About the Publisher

Accepting manuscripts in the most categories. We love to help people get their words available to the world.

Revival Waves of Glory focus is to provide more options to be published. We do traditional paperbacks, hardcovers, audio books and ebooks all over the world. A traditional royalty-based publisher that offers self-publishing options, Revival Waves provides a very author friendly and transparent publishing process, with President Bill Vincent involved in the full process of your book. Send us your manuscript and we will contact you as soon as possible.

Contact: Bill Vincent at rwgpublishing@yahoo.com www.rwgpublishing.com